Music Festivals and Concerts in Virtual Reality

The Ultimate Entertainment Evolution

Table of Contents

Chapter 1. Introduction

Welcome to the dawn of a new era in entertainment! If you thought that the progression from live performances to recorded music was revolutionary, then fasten your seatbelts because the thrilling world of Music Festivals and Concerts in Virtual Reality is here! Our special report will take you on a stunning journey through this trailblazing terrain, capturing the energy and vibrancy of live music events while offering unparalleled convenience and immersive experiences. Discover how this dynamic evolution of entertainment is breaking boundaries, redefining enjoyment, and expertly bridging the gap between global audiences and their favorite artists. So, ready to tune into the future alongside us? Grab a copy of our special report today and venture into how your future concert experiences are about to get a major, virtual upgrade!

Chapter 2. The Anatomy of Virtual Reality

At the core of the revolutionary entertainment epoch is the technical powerhouse - virtual reality, or VR. It isn't merely a buzzword or a flashy piece of gadgetry meant to dazzle audiences: it's a deeply transformative technology, shaping the form and nature of experiences in untold ways. To fully comprehend its impact on music festivals and concerts, we first need to delve into its anatomy and understand how it functions.

2.1. The Essence of VR

Virtual reality simulates an environment, creating an artificial sensory experience that can mimic real-world situations or conjure the fantastical. It's a multi-sensory experience involving sight, touch, hearing, and even smell. The most captivating aspect of VR is how it achieves a sense of presence. This term signifies the level of immersion an individual feels when they can perceive themselves existing within the virtual world. It's a profound and unsettlingly real experience that many find hard to describe.

VR's potency in delivering this sense of presence is largely due to the technology's simultaneous stimulation of various senses. By coordinating the information flowing to our senses, VR convinces our brains that the digital environment we're experiencing is indeed real.

2.2. VR Hardware: A Close Look

To successfully simulate the senses, VR employs a suite of hardware devices.

1. **Head-Mounted Display (HMD)**: The most identifiable piece of VR

equipment, the HMD, is worn on the head, displaying the virtual environment to the eyes. It tracks the user's head movements and adjusts the environment accordingly, enhancing the illusion of reality. Today's HMDs have high-resolution screens and wide fields of view to complement the immersive experience.

2. **Controllers**: These handheld devices capture your hand movements and translate them into actions within the virtual environment. Some advanced forms of controllers offer haptic feedback, replicating the sensation of touch.

3. **Motion Tracking Systems**: These track the user's body movements, often using "markers" that reflect light or send signals to a sensor. It allows the VR system to keep track of the user's physical location within the virtual space.

4. **Vestibular Stimulation Devices**: Though still experimental, these devices can replicate feelings of motion or "tactile" sensations in VR by directly stimulating specific parts of a user's nervous system.

2.3. VR Software: Creating Worlds

The hardware is only half of the VR puzzle. It's the software that renders the world, and this involves large amounts of data and intricate programming. Any virtual concert or music festival would need the combined efforts of 3D artists, sound designers, and software engineers to create not only the look and feel of the stage and performers but also the interaction mechanisms for audience members.

Managing a balance between graphical complexity and system performance is crucial. The virtual world needs to be visually stunning to enhance the feeling of presence, yet it also needs to run smoothly, minimizing delay between a user's actions and the system's response to maintain immersion.

2.4. The Networking Aspect

Virtual concerts and music festivals aren't solitary experiences, so there's also an immense networking component to consider. Thousands, if not hundreds of thousands of people can attend these events simultaneously.

VR systems must handle multiple streams of data while maintaining performance and coherence, allowing users to interact with each other in real-time, within the shared virtual space. This is where the concepts of cloud computing and edge computing come into play, helping to spread the computational and networking load.

2.5. Integration of VR with Music Festivals and Concerts

The integration of VR with music festivals and concerts will indeed redefine our entertainment experiences. Imagine never missing out on your favorite music festival due to travel restrictions or budget constraints. It offers unprecedented accessibility, reducing the gap between global audiences and artists. Concert-goers can enjoy performances in high-definition audio and video, with an immersive, 360-degree view of the stage, virtually exploring the venue at their leisure.

This high degree of personalization is what sets VR concerts apart. You have the freedom to choose your location within the gig, watch from different vantage points, and focus on particular members of the band; it's a unique experience for each person.

2.6. Conclusion

The possibility of experiencing concerts and music festivals in VR isn't a fantasy in a science-fiction novel. We're on the brink of this becoming a mainstream reality, offering an entirely new dimension to entertainment. By emphasizing interactivity and presence, VR has the potential to transform music experience from a passive activity into a dynamic, customizable, immersive journey. It's not merely about observing but becoming part of the experience, a far cry from the static screens of yesterday.

To be part of this dazzling future, it's important to understand how VR works and what it can offer. With advancements in both VR hardware and software, combined with increasing affordability, we are marching into a future where music is not just heard, but seen, felt, and lived in ways like never before.

Chapter 3. Rise of VR in Entertainment: A Brief History

The blending of entertainment and creativity often results in remarkable breakthroughs which have the potential to reinvent entire industries. One such game-changing advancement is the incorporation of Virtual Reality (VR) into various facets of the entertainment ecosystem, allowing for transformative and mesmerizing experiences. To appreciate the profundity of this revolution, let's delve into the origins and progression of VR's role in shaping entertainment as we know it today.

3.1. The Emergence of VR

The genesis of VR technology traces back to the mid-20th century, with early forms emanating from the sphere of computer graphics, visual simulations, and immersive multisensory experiences. The term "Virtual reality" itself was coined by Jaron Lanier in 1987, during the period of intense research, development, and public fascination.

The early applications of VR were predominantly focused on military, healthcare, and aviation sectors for training purposes. These industries recognized the potential that VR presented for detailed, complex, and safe simulations. However, the high costs and primitive technology meant the reach of VR was limited, and consumer applications remained largely unexplored.

3.2. The Dream of Virtual Entertainment

The concept of integrating VR into entertainment had been a prevalent theme, albeit largely confined within the realms of science fiction literature and films, before it was technologically feasible. The dream was to create a convincing, digitized reality capable of surpassing the borders of the physical world, allowing people to break away from their mundane routines and explore the uncharted territories of their imagination.

Movies like "The Lawnmower Man" in the early '90s and later, "The Matrix", presented an exhilarating vision of entertainment possibilities. Vivid depictions of characters indulging in seemingly real experiences in a digital world both thrilled and sparked the curiosity of audiences, setting the groundwork for the expectation and adoption of such technology in the future.

3.3. Early Reality vs. Virtual Reality in Entertainment

As the technology started to mature, VR began making inroads into the entertainment sector, initially via gaming. Companies like Atari established research labs to investigate VR's potential, while Sega and Nintendo made early attempts to launch VR products. Despite the resultant fanfare, these initiatives were commercially unsuccessful, largely attributed to the poor quality of the VR experiences. Technological limitations led to blocky graphics, high latency, low frame rates, and an overall absence of the much-anticipated immersion.

However, these initial forays provided valuable information for the evolution of VR. Developers recognized the need for more advanced graphics systems, responding controls, and user-friendly interfaces.

But perhaps most importantly, they began to focus on ways to provide a full immersion experience, understanding that this is what separates VR from conventional entertainment forms.

3.4. The Technological Renaissance and Modern VR

The resurrection of VR in general interest and its adoption in entertainment can primarily be attributed to two factors: the advancement in technology and the reintroduction of VR by companies like Oculus VR.

The development and miniaturization of components, the rise of mobile computing, advancements in graphics processing capabilities, and improvements in the design and comfort of head-mounted devices were all instrumental in giving VR technology a much-needed boost and eventual commercial viability.

In 2012, a Kickstarter campaign by Oculus VR indicated the renewed interest and faith in the technology. Their initial product, the Oculus Rift, promised and delivered an immersive and affordable VR experience. This sparked renewed interest, ushering in a wave of VR development and its application in the entertainment arena, lining up the likes of Sony, HTC, and Facebook in the race.

3.5. VR in Gaming: The First Success

The initial success story of VR in entertainment was undoubtedly within the realm of gaming. The gaming community, always hungry for innovations, embraced VR as it offered a departure from conventional flat-screen playing into a fully immersive, interactive, and visceral experience.

The likes of Full Dive Gaming that employs gesture tracking, positional tracking, and orientation tracking took games to new heights. The players were no longer just players but active participants within the game itself. Beyond this, game developers started focusing on VR-centric narrative techniques, bringing a new level of depth to the world of gaming.

3.6. The Transition to Music

While VR was making groundbreaking advancements in gaming, music enthusiasts and technologists realized its potential in recreating live concerts. This was a game-changing development, transcending geographical boundaries and enhancing the engagement of global audiences. The goal was no longer limited to just observing a performance, but to place the viewer right at the heart of the action, offer multiple vantage points, backstage access, or even the chance to interact with the artists.

3.7. Taking The Virtual Stage

Even though VR had shown promise in live performance applications, it was the global pandemic in 2020 that truly fast-tracked adoption. Social distancing and worldwide lockdowns created a need for virtual events. In response, major music festivals moved online, with artists performing to global audiences via live-streamed VR experiences. Large-scale events such as Tomorrowland and Marshmello's concert in Fortnite successfully attracted millions of viewers, demonstrating the potential reach and attraction for such experiences.

3.8. Current State and Future Potential

Today, VR is a buzzword throughout the entertainment industry, primarily driven by its recent successes in the music arena.

Companies such as Wave, MelodyVR, and Oculus are continually working to refine VR concert experiences, focusing on image resolution, audio quality, and interactive components to create experiences that are as good, if not better, than the real thing.

As we stand on the precipice of the next wave in entertainment, what remains certain is that VR has a significant role to play. It is poised to reshape the boundaries of entertainment, bringing immersive experiences not only to music and gaming but potentially extending to live sports, theater, movies, education, and beyond. There's a thrilling journey ahead, and it promises a reality like no other. As the curtain falls on this chapter, one thing is certain: the future of entertainment is virtually limitless.

Chapter 4. The Technology Behind VR Concerts and Festivals

Let's dive into the technological marvels that bring VR Concerts and Festivals to life, utterly transforming our music experiences.

4.1. Understanding Virtual Reality

Virtual Reality (VR) involves simulating a different reality to the one we are normally used to through high-quality audio and realistic images. It enables an encounter in a homemade circumstance or an entirely different world. To date, the primary utilization of VR technology has been in the gaming industry, but it's quickly extending to others, such as entertainment and music.

VR works through duplicating our senses like vision, hearing, touch and even smell to create an illusion of reality. The VR gadget, often a headset worn on the eyes like goggles, stimulates our senses in such a way that we experience the artificial world as real.

4.2. Hardware Utilized for VR Concerts

VR concerts utilize a standard set of VR hardware:

- **VR Headset:** The Head-Mounted Display (HMD) or VR headset plays a crucial role representing two screens, one in front of each eye. The lenses focus and reshape the image for each eye and create a stereoscopic 3D image by angling the two 2D images.

- **Audio:** Most VR headsets are equipped with headphones to fully immerse the user into the VR concert. Some also offer spatial sound to improve the experience further.

- **Motion tracking:** This is essential for creating a plausible reality. The system tracks the user's motion and adjusts the images accordingly.

- **Controller:** Utilized for hand-based interactions in the virtual environment.

The sophistication of this hardware, especially the motion tracking technology, makes a massive contribution to the realism and immersion of the VR concert experience.

4.3. Data Capture for VR Concerts

The data capture process for a VR concert is an elaborate affair, involving several steps:

- **Stage Mapping:** This process involves creating a virtual model of the stage where the concert is to take place.

- **Motion Capture:** The performers' movements are recorded using an extensive array of cameras and, sometimes, body suits embedded with sensors.

- **Audio Capture:** The audio is recorded using specially designed microphones that capture a full 360 degrees of sound, also known as "spatial audio."

- **Post-production:** Combining all the elements together to create the final, fully immersive product.

4.4. Producing VR Content

Creating VR content is quite complex, compared to other forms of media. Stages must be meticulously plotted out in 3D space, and the cameras used must record simultaneously, ensuring the seamless overlap of visual fields to create a convincing VR experience.

The captured footage is stitched together using software that synchronizes and blends the individual videos into one cohesive, spherical video. Advanced software algorithms work on smoothing out the borders between each camera viewpoint, ideally to the point where they become invisible, to produce a continuous and stable environment.

4.5. VR Concert Streaming

It's essential that users can access and take part in the VR experience easily, regardless of their geographical location. For this, a robust streaming technology is required. The process involves encoding the VR content into a format suitable for Internet streaming, transmitting it to the user's device, and decoding it for viewing.

Low-latency streaming is crucial for maintaining the realism and immersion of a virtual concert, making it seem as though the user is truly there in real time.

4.6. Future of VR in Music

As music concerts and festivals continue their migration to the digital realm, thanks to VR, the boundaries of what is possible are constantly being pushed. Future technologies might include haptic suits that enable the user to "feel" the music or the crowd's roar, or scent technology to provide specific smells associated with the real-life concert experience.

4.7. VR Concerts: Challenges & Opportunities

While the technology underpinning VR concerts is thrilling, it's not without its challenges. Creating quality VR content is still a complex and time-consuming process. It can also be expensive, which may put a financial strain on event organizers.

On the other hand, VR offers opportunities for music shows to become more inclusive and accessible to fans worldwide. It reduces the barriers of cost and physical distance, allowing fans to enjoy their favorite artists virtually from the comfort of their own homes.

In conclusion, the technology behind VR concerts and festivals has the potential to revolutionize the music industry. While there will undoubtedly be challenges along the way, the opportunities for greater audience reach, increased accessibility, incomparable immersive experiences, and more makes this a thrilling frontier in the world of entertainment. Embracing this technology and exploring its potential will be crucial for the future of music.

Chapter 5. Understanding the Audience: Who is Embracing Virtual Reality in Music

The first wave of adopters embracing Virtual Reality (VR) in music spans a diverse demographic, embracing technology early on to quench their thirst for innovative entertainment. This section offers a comprehensive understanding of who the primary consumers of this technology are, their characteristics, motivations, and what this may mean for the future of virtual reality events.

5.1. Age and Demographics of the VR Audience

While early adoption of new technology is often associated with the younger generations, interestingly VR in music isn't isolated to that stereotype. The appeal of virtual concerts stretches across several generations. The younger demographic, characterized by a thirst for advanced technology, are undeniably key players. Age groups ranging from 15 to 34, generally classified as Generation Z and the younger section of Millennials, are particularly prone to exploring these new experiences, driven by their inherent curiosity and sophisticated technology interfaces.

At the same time, older demographics are equally drawn to the allure of VR concerts. Age groups 35 and up, including older Millennials and Gen X, find this technology attractive, considering it eliminates the conventional hassles of attending a live concert, such as travel, accommodation, and concerns about personal safety in large crowds. Trust and comfort with online platforms play a crucial role in this adoption. In essence, the VR music audience is a blend of younger tech-savvy users and more mature technology users, seeking unique experiences or a hassle-free alternative to live concerts.

5.2. Geographic Distribution

Geographic distribution plays an interesting role in the adoption of VR for music. It's not reserved to technology hubs or developed countries but is seeing a global uptake. For instance, across North America and Europe, which are traditionally quick to adopt and develop new technology, VR platforms are making a splash in the music industry. In these regions, artists and music festivals are eagerly exploring VR possibilities to reach their fans.

Interestingly, Asian markets, particularly South Korea, Japan, and China, are surging ahead in this sphere. The momentum can be attributed to these countries' digital infrastructure, the strong presence of technology companies, and consumers with a notorious appetite for new tech. They view VR as another medium to consume content from beloved K-pop bands or international artists whose live concerts may not be geographically accessible.

5.3. Motivations of VR Audience

Understanding why audiences are attracted to VR in music provides key insights into what sparks the audience interest. One of the dominant motivations is the elevated element of immersion and interactivity. Fans can not only watch their favorite artists but also interact within the environment to a certain extent. This level of engagement often goes beyond what's possible in physical concerts.

Another fundamental motivator is convenience. The ability to enjoy a concert experience from the comfort of their home allows fans to eliminate issues such as expensive tickets, travel, and accommodation, venue overcrowding, and security concerns. Moreover, VR concerts offer a solution for those with mobility issues, allowing them to experience events they otherwise wouldn't be able to attend.

5.4. The Role of the Pandemic

The onset of the COVID-19 pandemic played an influential role in pushing both musicians and fans toward VR. The sudden halt of live performances sparked a rise in the adoption of VR as musicians sought new ways to connect with their fans and maintain income. At the same time, fans trapped at home due to lockdowns turned to VR concerts as an alternate means of entertainment. The pandemic leapfrogged VR concert technology by exposing a wider demographic to its potential.

5.5. Closing Thoughts

The audience for VR in music is as diverse as it is dynamic. Classifications are determined more by a shared interest in technology and music, rather than by age or geography. Understanding this eclectic audience's motivations and preferences is a crucial step in optimizing and expanding VR offerings in the concert scene.

As the technology continues to evolve and become more accessible, the demographic adopting it is expected to expand. Musicians and concert organizers can benefit from recognizing who their audience is and why they are choosing VR. Armed with this, they can effectively tailor and market their virtual events to resonate with the broad, unconventional, and enthusiastic user base.

Chapter 6. Case Studies: Breakthrough VR Concerts and Festivals

Tech giants, musicians, and concert organizers have been foraging grounds in Virtual Reality (VR) to explore new possibilities in entertainment. Immersing yourself in your favorite music festivals or concerts without leaving the comfort of your own space is no longer an unattainable dream. This chapter will take a magnifying glass to some of the most groundbreaking VR music events that have been realized to date, delineating precisely what made each event special and how they have contributed to setting the stage for the future of concerts and festivals.

6.1. The Wave Beta and Lindsey Stirling

We begin with the collaboration between the VR platform Wave Beta, and the eclectic violinist Lindsey Stirling. The concert, which took place in August 2019, offered a dynamic example of how VR could bring an otherworldly live performance directly into the living rooms of fans around the globe. Stirling's signature blend of classical violin and modern dance music was enhanced by fantastic transformations of the artist and the environment throughout the performance, creating an immersive landscape that would have been impossible in a physical show. These mesmerizing visuals, combined with the interactive capabilities of the Wave Beta platform, where audiences could interact not only with Stirling but also with each other in real-time, offered an intensely immersive experience that sent ripples through the entertainment industry.

6.2. Marshmello's Concert in Fortnite

Perhaps one of the most talked-about VR events was the virtual concert by DJ Marshmello within the sensational game space Fortnite. In 2019, the event set a new record with over 10 million concurrent attendees. The collaboration between Marshmello and Fortnite was groundbreaking from multiple perspectives. Not only did it demonstrate the significant potential that the gaming industry holds for musicians or artists, but it also underscored the power of VR to attract colossal audiences. Besides, the interactive in-game elements and choreographed dance breaks added an element of participation that imbued a sense of real concert environment.

6.3. Tomorrowland's Virtual Island Festival

The global pandemic of 2020 forced the world to observe strict social distancing measures, which inadvertently sparked an acceleration in the adoption of VR technologies. The famous Belgian electronic music festival Tomorrowland spearheaded this movement, launching its first-ever digital edition on a grand virtual 3D island, Pāpiliōnem. This festival presented an excellent example of how virtual events could seamlessly emulate the synesthetic experience of attending a live concert or festival. Attendees reveled in the four-day festival with eight different virtual stages, each boasting distinct, fully immersive environments. The interactive island setup fused the thrill of exploration with the energy of the iconic Tomorrowland performances, brimming with an array of exclusive artist sets.

6.4. New Orleans Jazz & Heritage Festival VR Experience

The 2020 VR celebration of the New Orleans Jazz & Heritage Festival highlighted not only the adaptability of VR technology but also its ability to combine education with entertainment. The free event provided visitors with interactive exhibits about the history of the Jazz & Heritage Festival. The spatial audio, coupled with the detailed museum-like presentations, recreated an ambiance of a cultural heritage site, thereby stressing the potential of VR in providing a holistic, educational experience.

6.5. Splendour XR: Splendour in the Grass's VR Debut

Finally, we turn our attention towards Splendour XR, the virtual edition of Australia's popular Splendour in the Grass music festival. This two-day event, which took place in July 2021, consolidated the power of the VR medium for the local music industry. With a global line-up of famous artists, the festival offered personalized avatars, exploration of a virtual world, and engaging interactions, reinstating the idea of globally accessible music fests.

Virtual Reality has revolutionized the way we experience music, with an increasing number of artists, festivals, and companies venturing into this field. Pioneers as those mentioned above are setting a new course for the concert and festival industry. Yet, while these case studies explore the potential of these powerful technologies, they also hint at the limitless potential that remains untapped. The convergence of technology and music has only just begun, and the chorus of this disruption is anticipated to play on a grander- and more immersive- scale in coming years.

Chapter 7. How VR is Transforming the Economics of the Music Industry

The recent advancements in virtual reality (VR) technology have disrupted numerous industries, pushing them to evolve in ways previously unimaginable. Perhaps no industry has felt the allure of this revolution more profoundly than the music industry. As it embraces VR's unprecedented capabilities, profound transformations are shaking its economic foundations, altering how revenues are generated and distributed.

7.1. The Paradigm Shift in Revenue Generation

In the traditional music industry, the bread-and-butter earnings mechanisms have been physical sales, digital downloads, concert tickets, merchandise sales, and licensing fees. Enter VR technology, and a whole new dimension of revenue generation emerges.

Virtual reality concerts and music experiences now allow fans from any location to attend live performances of their favorite artists, right from the convenience of their homes. They not only pay for an immersive experience but a proximity to the artists, an intimacy that the best physical concert seats can't provide. For example, virtual reality music platform MelodyVR reported an average revenue per user (ARPU) of $15 — much higher than other leading digital music platforms.

This represents not just an additional revenue stream, but possibly a new primary income source, especially as the technology matures and prices become more accessible to a broader audience.

7.2. The Democratization of the Live Experience

One of the most enduring draws of the music industry is the live concert experience. However, not everyone can attend these events due to geographical, physical, or financial restrictions. Thanks to VR, this is rapidly changing.

Through virtual concerts, fans can enjoy the live experience anytime, anywhere, breaking down the geographical boundaries. The personal VIP access granted by these virtual platforms can, at times, surpass the experience of being physically present at the concert. This democratization not only creates an entirely new customer base but changes the dynamics of ticket sales, making every 'seat' a potential front-row experience.

7.3. Redefining Music Production and Marketing

VR has also transformed the music production and marketing processes, offering an elaborate palette of creative possibilities to artists. Creating music specific to virtual reality environments or marketing music through VR experiences offers artists the ability to monetize their work like never before.

With VR, artists can collaborate in real-time, even if they're located at different geographical locations - therein creating possibilities of new kinds of music compositions and production. Release events of such collaborative projects, when conducted through VR, can pull in audiences from across the globe, expanding the specter of revenues dramatically.

7.4. Merchandising in the Virtual Realm

Merchandise sales have always been a significant revenue source for many artists and record labels. Embracing VR can enhance this further by offering virtual merchandise. Think virtual T-shirts, posters, and other paraphernalia — these can be created with far lower overhead costs and sold within the VR environments.

Virtual merchandise does not have to be limited to basic items – it can extend to virtually autographed items, virtual backstage passes, or even virtual self-portraits of the audience alongside their favorite artists. The possibilities are endless and only bounded by creativity.

7.5. Adding Depth to Fan Relationships

VR enables a new kind of fan-artist relationship, resulting in constructive revenue implications. Fans can now get 'exclusive access' to the backstage of concerts, intimate moments of creative processes, and even one-on-one interactions with artists. These experiences, unique to VR, are not only engaging but are premium services that can be monetized, creating active and continuous revenue streams.

7.6. An Evolving Business Model

The integration of VR into the music industry presents an evolution of the business model. Beside generating new revenue streams, VR also invites opportunities for partnerships with tech companies and brands. Sponsorships and advertisements within VR platforms present entirely new avenues for monetizing music contents.

In conclusion, the impact of VR on the economics of the music industry is profound. It adds a whole new dimension to the music industry's economic structure, introducing many possibilities for revenue generation. The full implications will become clear only as the technology continues to mature, and both artists and audiences become more comfortable and proficient at navigating and exploiting this new and exciting landscape. While we are still in the early phase of this transformation, it is already evident that VR provides an opportunity for the music industry to redefine its economic model in unprecedented ways.

Chapter 8. The Challenges: Understanding the Hurdles Virtual Reality Must Overcome

While the prospect of experiencing live music and concerts in a virtual reality (VR) environment is exhilarating, the path to making this a mainstream reality has several obstacles to overcome. From technical hurdles to perceptual misconceptions, let's dissect some of the significant challenges the industry must surmount on this ambitious quest.

8.1. Technological Limitations

One of the considerable hurdles to seamless VR concert experiences is the current state of technology. Processing power, resolution, latency, and interactivity capabilities need significant advancement to effectively replicate the real-life intensity and vibrancy of a music concert. Real-time rendering of high-quality visuals remains a challenge, as does the mimicry of sensory feedback, which is vital for a truly immersive experience.

Additionally, VR's capability to handle multitudes of concurrent users is still not up to the mark. A virtual concert attended by thousands of global participants may cause server overload, quality degradation, and buffering issues, souring an immersive experience into one fraught with frustration.

8.2. Accessibility Issues

Despite the declining costs, quality VR equipment needed for a superior virtual concert experience remains quite expensive. This cost factor could be an inhibiting factor in making such an experience universally accessible. A cost-effective, yet high-performing hardware solution is a prerequisite for bringing VR concerts to mainstream audiences.

Moreover, the interface and controls for virtual reality need to be user-friendly to engage a broader audience spectrum, including older individuals or those less technologically inclined. A steep learning curve stands as a potential deterrent to widespread VR adoption.

8.3. Health and Safety Concerns

Although VR provides transformative experiences, prolonged VR usage can have health implications. Users often report symptoms ranging from headaches to dizziness, disorientation, and even VR-induced motion sickness. These issues could deter enthusiasts from attending longer events like virtual concerts or music festivals.

Safety is another concern. With most VR headsets, users are visually isolated from their physical surroundings, creating potential risks. Creating a safe environment for users to enjoy VR experiences without compromising on immersion remains a challenge.

8.4. Sociocultural Barriers

Human beings are social creatures, and concerts have always served as a medium of communal enjoyment and shared experiences. The sense of togetherness and energy of a live crowd is hard to replicate virtually. Meeting this sociocultural expectation is a challenge VR concerts must overcome.

Furthermore, virtual reality's reputation has sometimes been tainted by perceptions of it as a solitary, antisocial activity. Rebranding the social image of VR and providing interconnected experiences that allow friends and people worldwide to share experiences in real-time can combat this stigma.

8.5. Business Models and Copyright Issues

Monetizing VR concerts, finding suitable business models, and ensuring sufficient returns for artists, event organizers, and VR platform providers can be a daunting endeavor. VR concerts should be priced at a point where they remain attractive to customers but also provide sufficient return on investment. They will also need to resist piracy, which is an ubiquitous issue in the digital arena.

In addition to these, issues around copyright and intellectual property protection are significant challenges. In a VR setting where users can potentially manipulate the digital space, regulation of content can be problematic.

8.6. Adapting Concerts to the Virtual Format

Curating and producing a live concert for the virtual realm is a unique challenge in itself. Concert experiences are typically multi-sensory engagements that heavily rely on the physical environment. Adapting these concerts to suit the virtual setting without diluting the intensity is an art yet to be mastered. Ensuring high-quality audio, interactive elements, and visuals that complement the music is crucial, but also challenging.

In conclusion, while the emergence of virtual reality concerts is a thrilling prospect, it's clear that significant challenges remain in making this a mainstream reality. That said, the relentless pace of technological innovation and the industry's drive to conquer these barriers paint a hopeful picture of the future. Indeed, the day may not be too far off when we'll be grabbing our VR headsets, meeting friends virtually, and rocking out to our favorite bands in exquisitely crafted digital concert halls.

Chapter 9. Potential Impact on Artists and Performers

Entertainment industries across the globe are continually evolving, exploring new frontiers to deliver visually, auditorially, and emotionally stunning experiences. At the forefront of this change is the application of Virtual Reality (VR), a technology that promises unprecedented immersion and enhancement in the domain of live music concerts. And while the implications for attendees are strikingly clear and exciting, there's a lot to discern about the potential impact on a different, but equally important group of stakeholders: the artists and performers themselves.

9.1. The Transformative Potential

Imagine that you're a musician. Traditionally, your performance and interaction with your audience were limited by physical constraints. The stage, the acoustics of the venue, the distance from the farthest fan - all these intricacies had to be considered. But with VR, those boundaries start to dissolve, enabling artists to construct extraordinary, imaginative concert experiences, unhindered by the usual limitations.

The concept revolves around the idea of putting the VR user directly into the venue. From a relaxed, intimate small bar show to a charismatic, full-throttle stadium gig, artists can replicate the entire spectrum and beyond in the virtual world, inviting their fans from across the globe to be a part of it.

This ability to design their performances can press the gears of creativity, thereby reshaping how artists approach concerts. The stage can shift from a static, physical construct to a dynamic, fluid entity, taking shapes beyond our wildest dreams. Artists can potentially perform against a backdrop of the milky way, in a jungle, or atop a moving train! The notion of the impossible starts to lose its meaning, enhancing the expressive power to the hands of the artists.

9.2. Empowerment of New Artists

The intricacies of physical geography have traditionally been a limiting factor for new artists. Local bands often struggle for visibility outside their own towns and cities. However, with the outreach potential of VR, this could all change.

New artists can capitalize on VR to bridge distances and bring their unique talent straight to a global audience. Instead of continually touring and playing at small local venues, artists can invest in one, well-produced virtual concert, making them instantly accessible to fans worldwide. Additionally, with potential integrations of social media within the VR space, they can directly engage with the audience, sharing their stories and establishing a stronger bond. This democratization of exposure can pave the way for more recognition, thereby providing a stepping-stone to success for new talents.

9.3. A More Sustainable Approach

Touring is an integral part of musicians' careers, but it's also physically draining and has a significant environmental impact due to travel and logistical necessities. Virtual concerts could offer a more sustainable model. Artists can reach their fans worldwide in real-time without leaving home. Yet they can create a sense of intimacy that even a packed stadium would struggle to match. The reduction in travel also means lesser carbon emissions, making for a more environmentally friendly mode of performance. This shift doesn't suggest the end of in-person concerts, but rather a supplementary approach that encompasses global reach and sustainability.

9.4. Enhancing Revenue Streams

The VR domain also carries promising implications when it comes to revenue generation for artists. Accessibility for live concerts is confined by venue size and ticket availability. However, virtual concerts can accommodate millions, widening the scope for ticket sales. Moreover, artists have the chance to offer their fanbase exclusive experiences, such as backstage passes, meet-and-greet scenarios, or front-row viewing experiences, all within VR. These unique, immersive experiences, which would be logistically challenging and exorbitantly priced in the real world, can become readily accessible and affordable in the VR experience, generating additional income.

9.5. Future Challenges and Considerations

While the potential benefits of VR in concerts are immense, it is also crucial to identify potential hurdles. Technological literacy among artists and audiences, the cost of VR equipment, and the need for high-speed internet access could be significant barriers to entry in the initial stages.

Moreover, artists have to redesign their craft to fit the VR model. They have to learn to interact with an audience they can't see and communicate within a digital framework that's very different from traditional concerts. There's also the risk of excessive digitization diluting the raw, organic nature of live performances - an essence that many concert-goers value deeply.

In conclusion, the realm of VR provides a captivating landscape for artists and performers. From demolishing geographical barriers to setting a stage for their wildest imaginations, VR is potentially a revolution waiting to happen in the music concert industry. New revenue models and sustainable practices accompany these possibilities, painting an appealing future. However, it would be wise not to overlook the challenges and plan implementations carefully, keeping a balancing act between tradition and innovation. Thus, artists need to tune themselves to this rhythm of change, for in this ambiguous dance of technology and talent, lies the future of musical performances.

Chapter 10. The Future of Virtual Concerts: Predictions and Trends

In the decade preceding the 2020s, few could have guessed the seismic shifts that were about to turn the world of entertainment on its head. Concerts drawing immense crowds - an empyrean powerhouse of noise, light, and energy - took a back seat to virtual concerts as the global pandemic turned the world off-stage.

Now, we find ourselves on the cusp of a new era. An era that celebrates virtual presence, as much as, if not more than, physical audience. But what does the future hold for such engagements? What will be the trends defining virtual concerts and how will they improve or disrupt the conventional music industry?

10.1. Global Accessibility Will Define the Future

The traditional setup of concerts poses several barriers, including geographic, economic, and sensory. Thousands of fans miss out on live performances because of prohibitive ticket costs, travel expenses, or other logistical challenges. Changes are imminent, however, and the global accessibility made possible by VR concerts sits at the center of it.

With virtual reality, the experience of immersive concert attendance is no longer restricted to a stadium or an arena. Instead, it has burst forth, gatecrashing into your homes, and shatterproofing the barriers of distance. In the comfort of your living room, you can enjoy a concert happening thousands of miles away, feeling the presence, energy, and music as if you were there in person.

In future, we predict VR concerts will bring about a new global village in the realm of music, where fans around the world connect, not only with the music and artists but also with each other as part of a global audience.

10.2. The Democratization of Music Festivals

Music festivals have been lauded as a melting pot of cultures, creative ingenuity, and fan fervor. However, the exorbitant costs, coupled with geographical constraints, have often turned these festivals into exclusive events, inaccessible to the broader public.

As a natural extension of the global accessibility, VR concerts can democratize music festivals. Technological innovations will make it possible to include fans irrespective of where they live or how much they earn. This new level of inclusivity will foster a stronger bond between artists and fans, fueling a global music community that transcends borders.

10.3. Redefining Concert Experiences Through Interactivity

Interactivity is a critical aspect of any live event. However, in traditional concerts, interactivity is limited due to crowd size and logistical issues.

This will change with virtual reality. The future of VR concerts is likely to include robust interactive features that allow fans to engage with the artists and their fellow audience in real-time. Concert-goers will have opportunities to vote on setlists, customize their avatars, and create an experience tailored to their preferences.

10.4. Creation of New Revenue Streams

Concert revenue today comes primarily from ticket sales, merchandise and refreshments, sponsor advertisements, and donations. In the future, VR concerts will usher in a diverse range of innovative revenue streams. These could include virtual merchandise, which fans can display or use in the virtual world, premium VR concert experiences like backstage passes or virtual meet and greets, micro-transactions for digital souvenirs, and much more.

10.5. Shaping the Future Through Sustainability

As concerts go virtual, the vast amounts of resources traditionally used in setting up live music events—including power, transport, and waste management—will be significantly reduced.

Virtual concerts are thus expected to forge a sustainable path for the music industry, helping tackle climate change concerns while entertaining global audiences. They offer an eco-friendly alternative to traditional events, helping reduce the carbon footprint of the music industry while still ensuring fans don't miss out on the enjoyment of live music.

Is it then a question of 'if' these changes will happen or 'when?' The narrative is rapidly evolving with artists like Travis Scott, The Weeknd, BTS and others pioneering the space. The pivot to VR concerts is happening right before our eyes, and the trends discussed above are rapidly becoming reality. But the true magic of this revolution lies in its endless possibilities, a symphony still tuning, orchestrated by the creativity of artists and the pulse of music lovers worldwide.

And as it rings out in full resonance, we can only reiterate, the future is here. And it's wearing a VR headset.

Chapter 11. Stepping into the Future: How to Experience VR Concerts Today

The first time you put on a VR headset and launch a concert experience, it feels like you're entering an alternate universe. The moment the 360-degree view kicks in and you find yourself standing in a crowd of virtual festival-goers, staring at a stage where your favorite band is performing live, you realize that this is a game-changer for the music industry.

11.1. Getting the Right Equipment

The first thing you need to take a step into the future and experience a VR concert is the right equipment. Not all headsets are created equal, and the one you choose can significantly affect your experience.

A higher-end device, such as the Oculus Rift, HTC Vive or PlayStation VR, will give you the best visual and auditory experience, but they require a high-performance computer or a specific game console to function.

On the other end of the spectrum, there are standalone devices like the Oculus Quest and mid-range devices like the Samsung Gear VR that require only a compatible smartphone. While less expensive, these options might not offer the same degree of immersion and visual quality as their higher-end counterparts.

11.2. Navigating the VR Concert Platforms

Once you have your hardware sorted, the next step is exploring the various VR concert platforms. Companies like MelodyVR, Wave, NextVR, and TheWaveVR are some of the top players currently offering immersive concert experiences in virtual reality.

These platforms feature a wide range of content, from on-demand concerts of popular artists to live gigs and other music-driven VR experiences.

Once you've chosen and installed a platform, navigating through the interface is simply a matter of learning how to move your head and hands in the VR space. Most platforms will provide tutorials on how to use their interface.

11.3. Choosing the Perfect View

One of the biggest advantages of VR concerts is the ability to choose your vantage point. You're no longer restricted to the seats you paid for or how early you queued. In most VR concert platforms, you'll have access to multiple viewing points: from front-row views to aerial perspectives, and even on stage with the band in some cases.

Take your time to explore the different viewpoints available during your VR concert experience – this freedom is part of what makes VR concerts so extraordinary.

11.4. Engaging Beyond Watching: Virtually Participate

But VR concerts aren't just about watching performances. They're about participation. With the advent of interactive vr-concerts, virtual audience members can cheer, dance, and get noticed by the performers - just like at a real show.

Wave and TheWaveVR lead the way in this kind of audience engagement, allowing users to create a unique avatar that can dance, interact with other concert-goers, and react to the music through different animations.

11.5. Ensuring High-Quality Internet Connection

Any real-time streaming, including VR concerts, require a good internet connection to prevent lags and breakdowns. A wired connection will be the most stable, but if you are using a wireless option, just ensure that you're close to the router.

11.6. Enjoying the Immersion and Blueprints For Socializing

Just like in a physical concert where the energy of the crowd is infectious, VR platforms are developing ways to create virtual photo pits or digital lounges for fans to connect with each other.

These social features might vary from platform to platform and will evolve with the technology, but they could include shared experiences like group watching, chat functions, or even in-app social media links.

11.7. A Greener and More Accessible Alternative

One final aspect that must be considered is the accessibility and sustainability of VR concerts. They have the potential to democratize concert attendance, breaking down geographical and financial barriers.

Moreover, virtual concerts reduce the carbon footprint associated with live events – no travel emissions, no waste from food and beverage consumption, and no need for massive energy-consuming sets.

Even when 'actual' live music events return in full force, VR concerts can continue to complement them, offering something uniquely immersive and powerful – an intimate, front-row view of your favourite musicians, from wherever you are in the world.

VR doesn't just represent the future – it's here, and it's now. It's time we adapt, learn, and embrace this new world of entertainment. As the virtual curtain falls, your applause echoes in your living room, and you remove your headset, you'll start to realize that you've just had a glimpse of the future of concerts, music festivals – indeed, a new era in entertainment itself. So get your VR headset ready, because your next concert could be happening right in your living room.